Encounters with God

The Gospel of LUKE

Encounters with God Study Guide Series

The Gospel of Matthew
The Gospel of Mark
The Gospel of Luke
The Gospel of John
The Acts of the Apostles
The Book of Romans

Encounters with God

The Gospel of LUKE

Copyright © 2007 by

Henry Blackaby, Th.M., D.D.
Richard Blackaby, M.Div., Ph.D.
Thomas Blackaby, M.Div., D.Min.
Melvin Blackaby, M.Div., Ph.D.
Norman Blackaby, M.Div., B.L., Ph.D.

Published by Thomas Nelson, Inc., P.O. Box 141000, Nashville, Tennessee 37214.

Scripture quotations are taken from The New King James Version® (NKJV), copyright 1979, 1980, 1982, 1992 Thomas Nelson, Inc., Publishers.

Library of Congress Cataloging-in-Publication Data
ISBN 1-4185-26401 9781418526405

Printed in the United States of America

07 08 09 10 RRD 9 8 7 6 5 4 3 2 1

CONTENTS

Contents

AN INTRODUCTION TO THE GOSPEL OF LUKE

The Gospel of Luke is the third book of the New Testament. It is the only Gospel account addressed to a specific individual, identified as Theophilus in the third verse of the book. The book is a narrative based upon eyewitnesses to the life and ministry of Jesus. It is the first of two books Luke wrote—the second and sequel is the Book of the Acts of the Apostles.

A Gospel Account. Luke is a Gospel account—one of four books in the New Testament labeled *Gospels*. It joins Matthew, Mark, and John as a book that is *all about Jesus*—what He did, what He said, and who He was and is. The word *gospel* literally means *good news*. The good news for Luke was that Jesus came to bring redemption to all people—not just the Jews, and not just to one segment of society.

Theophilus is addressed as *most excellent* (Luke 1:3), a term generally reserved for Roman officials. He is clearly a Gentile, with a Gentile name. His name in the Greek language literally means *lover of God*, and Luke may have been writing to all Gentile believers or to a particular community. Either way, the Gospel of Luke is aimed at confirming with *certainty* the truth about Jesus—that He is the Savior of all (Luke 1:4). Individuals from all ethnic and socioeconomic groups, both men and women, can find salvation in Him.

A Synoptic Gospel. Luke is one of the three *synoptic* Gospels, along with Matthew and Mark. The word *synoptic* means *seeing from one viewpoint* or *one overview*. Luke, Matthew, and Mark cover many of the same incidents and messages of Jesus in their Gospel accounts. In many ways, their accounts are similar to three photograph albums taken by three different photographers covering essentially the same life and events. Just as each photographer has a unique vantage point, angle, and composition, so each of the synoptic Gospels has a distinct voice, style, and purpose. Each Gospel, however, has a tone, pace, and emphasis that is unique.

Perhaps the foremost word to describe the Gospel of Luke is *compassion*. Luke overflows with gracious and lovely expressions of grace. It has been called the most beautiful book in the Bible.

The Gospel of Luke presents a selective history of Jesus' life, for the purpose of conveying a theological message: God offers salvation to all who will accept Christ Jesus as their Savior. Samaritans, Gentiles, publicans, sinners, and those shunned by society are offered redemption by God through Christ. Luke draws attention to Christ's mercy toward the outcasts, the vulnerable, and the despised. God's nature is revealed as compassionate, gentle, and caring—not wanting anyone to perish in their sin, but rather, inviting all to experience the abundant life He intends for them to have. Jesus deals lovingly with children, women, the diseased, those trapped in sin, and those who are considered by many to be beyond redemption.

Many Bible historians and scholars believe Luke was writing to encourage Gentile believers who may have had questions about the Jewish origins of the faith, or who may have desired confirmation that they were totally acceptable to God. Luke may also have been writing to confirm to Roman authorities that Christianity posed no political threat to Rome, but rather, was a force for love and peace in Roman society. At the time Luke wrote his Gospel, there does not appear to have been a Gospel account circulating widely among the Gentile churches. (Mark was written specifically for the church in Rome; Matthew was written for Jewish believers.) Luke wrote his Gospel to provide a full and accurate record about *all that Jesus began both to do and to teach until the day he was taken up* to heaven (Acts 1:1–2).

Among the prominent themes or concepts in the Gospel of Luke are the Kingdom of God, the Holy Spirit, and prayer.

The Gospel of Luke is the longest book in the New Testament. The bulk of the narrative is devoted to Jesus' miracles and parables. Some of the best-known and most-loved stories and parables of Jesus are found in Luke. It is a book filled with joy!

Luke the Author. Although Luke never identifies himself as the author of this book, church tradition from the earliest days identifies him as the author. Luke, short for Lucanus, was the physician and traveling companion of the apostle Paul (Philemon 1:24 and 2 Timothy 4:11). Paul refers to Luke as *beloved*, indicating the closeness of their relationship (See Colossians 4:14.). Luke is clearly aware of Jewish traditions and customs, and he may have been a Jew, although most believe he was a Gentile convert.

Many Bible scholars believe Luke interviewed eyewitnesses to the life and ministry of Jesus as he traveled with Paul, and that he especially set out to document the life of Jesus during the time Paul was imprisoned in Caesarea and Rome, perhaps hoping his account would aid Paul in his defense.

As a physician, Luke writes in an orderly, almost scientific manner, at the same time demonstrating a special interest in Jesus' healing miracles.

An Overview of Our Study
of the Gospel of Luke

This study guide presents seven lessons drawn from the Gospel of Luke. The study guide elaborates on the commentary included in the *Blackaby Study Bible*:

Lesson #1: God Works through Ordinary Lives

Lesson #2: Jesus Calls Ordinary People to Follow Him

Lesson #3: Jesus Heals and Delivered All Who Came to Him

Lesson #4: Jesus Has Compassion on Sinners and Outcasts

Lesson #5: Jesus Emphasizes Love and Forgiveness to All

Lesson #6: Jesus Seeks Out All Who are Lost

Lesson #7: Jesus Teaches Faithfulness and Watchfulness

Personal or Group Use. These lessons are offered for personal study and reflection or for small-group Bible study. The questions may be answered by an individual reader or used as a foundation for group discussion. A section titled "Notes to Leaders of Small Groups" is included at the back of this book to help those who might lead a group study of the material.

Before you embark on this study, we encourage you to read in full "How to Study the Bible" in the *Blackaby Study Bible* on pages viii–ix. Our contention is always that the Bible is unique among all literature. It is God's definitive word for humanity. The Bible is

- *inspired*—God breathed

- *authoritative*—absolutely the final word on any spiritual matter

- *the plumb line of truth*—the standard against which all human activity and reasoning must be evaluated

The Bible is fascinating in that it has remarkable diversity, but also perfect unity. The books were penned by a diverse assortment of authors representing a variety of languages and cultures. The Bible as a whole has a number of literary forms. But, the Bible's message from cover to cover is clear, consistent, and unified.

More than mere words on a page, the Bible is an encounter with God Himself. No book is more significant to your life. The very essence of the Bible is the Lord Himself.

God speaks by the Holy Spirit through the Bible. He also communicates during your time of prayer, in your life circumstances, and through His church. Read your Bible in an attitude of prayer and allow the Holy Spirit to make you aware of God's activity in and through your personal life. Write down what you learn, meditate on it, and adjust your thoughts, attitudes, and behavior accordingly. Look for ways every day in which the truth of God's Word can be applied to your circumstances and relationships. God is not random, but orderly and intentional in the way He speaks to you.

Be encouraged—the Bible is *not* too difficult for the average person to understand if that person asks the Holy Spirit for help. (Furthermore, not even the most brilliant person can fully understand the Bible apart from the Holy Spirit's help!) God desires for you to know Him and to know His Word. Everyone who reads the Bible can learn from it. The person who will receive maximum benefit from reading and studying the Bible, however, is the one who:

- *is born again* (John 3:3, 5). Those who are born again and have received the gift of God's Spirit have a distinct advantage in understanding the deeper truths of His Word.

- *has a heart that desires to learn God's truth*. Your attitude greatly influences the outcome of Bible study. Resist the temptation to focus on what others have said about the Bible. Allow the Holy Spirit to guide you as you study God's Word for yourself.

- *has a heart that seeks to obey God*. The Holy Spirit teaches most those who have a desire to apply what they learn. Begin your Bible study with prayer, asking the Holy Spirit to guide your thoughts and to impress upon you what is on God's heart. Then, make plans to adjust your life immediately to obey the Lord fully.

As you read and study the Bible, your purpose is not to *create* meaning, but to *discover* the meaning of the text with the Holy Spirit's guidance. Ask yourself, "What did the author have in mind? How was this applied by those who first heard these words?" Especially in your study of the Gospel accounts, pay attention to the words of Jesus that begin "Most assuredly" or "He opened His mouth and taught them, saying." These are core principles and teachings that powerfully impact every person's life.

At times you may find it helpful to consult other passages of the Bible (made available in the center columns in the *Blackaby Study Bible*) or the commentary in the margins of the *Blackaby Study Bible*.

Keep in mind always that Bible study is not primarily an exercise for acquiring information, but it is an opportunity for transformation as you meet God face to face. Bible study is your opportunity to encounter God and to be changed in His presence. When God speaks to your heart, nothing remains the same. Jesus said, "He who has ears to hear, let him hear" (Matthew 13:9). Choose to have ears that desire to hear!

The B-A-S-I-Cs of Each Study in This Guide. Each lesson in this study guide has five segments, using the word BASIC as an acronym. The word BASIC does not allude to elementary or simple, but rather to *foundational*. These studies extend the concepts that are part of the *Blackaby Study Bible* commentary and are focused on key aspects of what it means to be a Christ-follower in today's world. The BASIC acronym stands for:

B = *Bible Focus.* This segment presents the central passage for the lesson and a general explanation that covers the central theme or concern.

A = *Application for Today.* This segment has a story or illustration related to modern-day times, with questions that link the Bible text to today's issues, problems, and concerns.

S = *Supplementary Scriptures to Consider.* In this segment, other Bible verses related to the general theme of the lesson are explored.

I = *Introspection and Implications.* In this segment, questions are asked that lead to deeper reflection about one's personal faith journey and life experiences.

C = *Communicating the Good News.* This segment presents challenging questions aimed at ways in which the truth of the lesson might be lived out and shared with others (either to win the lost or build up the church).

Lesson #1

GOD WORKS
THROUGH ORDINARY LIVES

*Obedience: doing what is requested
by a higher authority without
question or delay*

B
Bible Focus

> *Now in the sixth month the angel Gabriel was sent by God to a city of Galilee named Nazareth, to a virgin betrothed to a man whose name was Joseph, of the house of David. The virgin's name was Mary. And having come in, the angel said to her, "Rejoice, highly favored one, the Lord is with you; blessed are you among women!"*
>
> *But when she saw him, she was troubled at his saying, and considered what manner of greeting this was. Then the angel said to her, "Do not be afraid, Mary, for you have found favor with God. And behold, you will conceive in your womb and bring forth a Son, and shall call His name JESUS. He will be great, and will be called the Son of the Highest; and the Lord God will give Him the throne of His father David. And He will reign over the house of Jacob forever, and of His kingdom there will be no end."*
>
> *Then Mary said to the angel, "How can this be, since I do not know a man?"*
>
> *And the angel answered and said to her, "The Holy Spirit will come upon you, and the power of the Highest will over- shadow you; therefore, also, that Holy One who is to be born will be called the Son of God. Now indeed, Elizabeth your relative has also conceived a son in her old age; and this is now the sixth month for her who was called barren. For with God nothing will be impossible."*
>
> *Then Mary said, "Behold the maidservant of the Lord! Let it be to me according to your word." And the angel departed from her (Luke 1:26–38).*

Mary the mother of Jesus is someone of prominence in the Christian world today. As a young teenager in the blue-collar town of Nazareth in the first century, she was a no one of importance. She had no status, except as the betrothed wife-to-be of a man named Joseph, who apparently was also very ordinary, at least as far as religious and social status was conferred from the theological headquarters of Jerusalem.

What Mary possessed was a lineage that went back to King David, purity as a virgin, and a heart willing to believe and trust God without regard to circumstance.

When the angel Gabriel appeared to Mary with the startling news that she had found favor with God, his first word to her was *Rejoice!* This is a word that rings throughout the Gospel of Luke. Those who live in relationship with Jesus Christ have a wellspring of inner joy. *Joy*, of course, is not linked to circumstances or situations as the more fleeting emotion of *happiness* tends to be. Joy is abiding. It comes from the inner core of a person and endures regardless of what is done or said by others. Joy comes when we truly know we have favor with God and we are in a position for Him to bless us and be considered valuable and useful.

The angel Gabriel gave impossible news to Mary—she was going to conceive a child by the Holy Spirit and bear a son who, as the Son of God, would be the greatest man who had ever lived. He would establish a kingdom that would last throughout eternity. Even as Gabriel gave her this impossible news, he assured Mary, *"with God, nothing will be impossible"* (Luke 1:37).

Many people given such incredible, awesome news in today's world might be skeptical, and with good reason!." Mary, in sharp contrast, says, "Behold the maidservant of the Lord! Let it be to me according to your word" (Luke 1:38).

In making this response, Mary sent a message of tremendous value to every person who will ever hear a call from God: "I believe. I believe God can do anything He desires to do. I believe *nothing* is impossible. I'm willing to obey, and to do whatever He asks of me."

Are you facing what appear to be impossible circumstances or problems that seems to have no solution? It is important that you too trust God to show you the answer and then act as He directs

Are you feeling as if you are a no one, and that nothing you do can make a difference for God in this world? It is important to see yourself as a servant of the Lord who is available for His use.

Faith to believe.

A heart to obey.

That is what God asks of each Christian today. It is all that is required for Him to create in you a unique opportunity to present Christ in your world.

A
Application for Today

She was a no one. As a sixteen-year-old, she had run away from her home in the middle part of the United States during the fifties, intent on becoming a movie star in Hollywood. Like most who dreamed her dream, she never made it to the big screen. Rather, she worked as a waitress until she discovered she could make a little more by selling her body on the streets. She then learned she could add to her income by selling marijuana on the side. By the time she was in her mid-twenties, she had been arrested and charged and convicted and jailed and released from jail at least a half dozen times.

Then someone told her Jesus loved her and could wipe clean the slate of her past. The person invited her to receive Jesus as her Savior and she did. That same person gave her a New Testament, and a new dress, and invited her to come to church.

No one in the church knew about her past. They didn't ask and she didn't tell. She attended church every Sunday morning and night, and started going to a Sunday school class and then to the Wednesday night prayer service. What people did notice was that more and more strangers started coming to the church. More and more people were responding to the pastor's altar calls to receive Jesus Christ as Savior. Some of those who came to the church were real down-and-outers, but over time, they lived changed lives. When people asked them how they heard about the church, they almost all pointed to her and said, "She told us we should come."

The pastor was grateful for the increased attendance, and the increased number of people receiving Jesus as Savior. He decided to talk to the young woman about her evangelism methods. He thought perhaps others could do what she was doing.

"What do you say to people to get them to come to church?" the pastor asked her one afternoon.

The young woman shrugged. "Not much," she said. "I wish I knew more to say. I work in a store as a cashier. When I see people who are messed up, and I'm handing them their change, I say, 'Here's your change. You know, I was really messed up not very long ago and Jesus changed me. If you ever want *real* change, Jesus can do it.'" She giggled a little as she added, "It is all about change, right?"

The pastor asked, "Do you invite them to church?"

"Sometimes," she said. "But what usually happens is that one day they'll come back into the store and ask me, 'How did Jesus do it?' I know what they mean. I tell them to come to church and *you'll* tell them how Jesus changes things. And then I say, whatever that preacher tells you to do, you do it. Jesus put him there to help you."

The young woman may not have called herself a woman of great faith. She may not have thought she was being supremely obedient to God. But the pastor knew she was both. And so did God.

How do you present Christ in *your* world?

S
Supplementary Scriptures to Consider

Elizabeth, a kinswoman of Mary, was beyond normal child-bearing years when the Lord told her husband, Zacharias, she would become pregnant. The angel Gabriel revealed Elizabeth's pregnancy to Mary, and Mary immediately sought out Elizabeth, even though they lived miles apart:

> "Now Mary arose in those days and went into the hill country with haste, to a city of Judah, and entered the house of Zacharias and greeted Elizabeth. And it happened, when Elizabeth heard the greeting of Mary, that the babe leaped in her womb; and Elizabeth was filled with the Holy Spirit. Then she spoke out with a loud voice and said, "Blessed are you among women, and blessed is the fruit of your womb! But why is this granted to me, that the mother of my Lord should come to me? For indeed, as soon as the voice of your greeting sounded in my ears, the babe leaped in my womb for joy. Blessed is she who believed, for there will be a fulfillment of those things which were told her from the Lord" (Luke 1:39–45).

• When you are faced with a new challenge, it is important to seek out the advice and encouragement of someone who has *been there, done that.* How important is it for new believers to be in close fellowship with more mature believers?

• Have other people, ideally more mature believers, called you *blessed*? If so what were the circumstances?

• Reflect upon this statement: "Blessed is she who believed, for there will be a fulfillment of those things which were told her from the Lord." Can you cite an example from your life of how your believing was linked to a fulfillment of things the Lord had spoken to your heart? What happens if we don't believe? Do we stop the fulfillment, or do we fail to recognize the fulfillment? Do we stop the blessing that accompanies believing?

It was customary in Mary's time for newly pregnant young women to spend time apart from their immediate families and daily chores in order to sing or speak to the baby developing in their wombs. A mother was considered to have a vital role in the spiritual formation of her baby. Part of their message or song was to be a response of joy about the pregnancy, and part of the message or song was intended to be a statement of belief regarding the future of the child. Luke gives us Mary's pregnancy song:

> And Mary said:
> "My soul magnifies the Lord,
>   And my spirit has rejoiced in God my Savior.
>   For He has regarded the lowly state of His maidservant;
>   For behold, henceforth all generations will call me blessed.
>   For He who is mighty has done great things for me,
>   And holy is His name.
>   And His mercy is on those who fear Him
>   From generation to generation.
>   He has shown strength with His arm;
>   He has scattered the proud in the imagination of their hearts.
>   He has put down the mighty from their thrones.
>   And exalted the lowly.
>   He has filled the hungry with good things,
>   And the rich He has sent away empty.
>   He has helped his servant Israel,
>   In remembrance of His mercy.
>   As He spoke to our fathers,
>   To Abraham and to his seed forever" (Luke 1:46–55).

• Reflect on ways Jesus fulfilled what Mary prophesied in her song.

• What does it mean to you for a person's soul to *magnify* the Lord? How have *you* magnified the Lord?

After the birth and naming of John (the Baptist), son of Elizabeth and Zacharias, the elderly first-time father uttered this prophecy:

> Now his father Zacharias was filled with the Holy Spirit,
> and prophesied, saying:
> "Blessed is the Lord God of Israel,
> For He has visited and redeemed His people,
> And has raised up a horn of salvation for us
> In the house of His servant David,
> As He spoke by the mouth of His holy prophets,
> Who have been since the world began,
> That we should be saved from our enemies
> And from the hand of all who hate us,
> To perform the mercy promised to our fathers
> And to remember His holy covenant,
> The oath which He swore to our father Abraham:
> To grant us that we,
> Being delivered from the hand of our enemies,
> Might serve Him without fear,
> In holiness and righteousness before Him all the days of our
> life" (Luke 1:67–75).

The blessing of a father on his children has been held in extremely high value since the earliest days of the Jewish patriarchs. (Read the prophetic blessings of Jacob on his sons and two of his grandsons in Genesis 48:15–16; 49.)

How did Zacharias speak blessing to John the Baptist?

Do you believe the spiritual opinion of your father has had a role in your spiritual development and life's work? In what ways? What difference can a blessing make in a child's life?

I
Introspection and Implications

1. What is your joy level? How do you maintain joy in the face of impossible conditions or odds?

2. Would you classify yourself as a no one or a someone? Do you know why? What does God say?

3. Whose spiritual opinion do you value most? How often do you check in with that person in your day to day decisions?

4. If you were writing a statement of blessing on your child, or a child you love dearly, what would you say? Take time to write that blessing and consider giving it to the child in the near future.

5. Reflect on the phrase in Zacharias's prophecy: "Grant us that we, being delivered from the hand of our enemies, might serve Him without fear, in holiness and righteousness before Him all the days of our life" (Luke 1:74–75). How can fear of others limit our ability to serve God fully? What does it mean to you to serve God in *holiness and righteousness*? Is this only for people especially called of God to fulfill unique or important roles, or are we *all* called by God to fulfill unique roles that are important in His kingdom?

C
Communicating the Good News

Is it a priority in your life to tell those who don't know Jesus Christ as their Savior and Lord that God values *all* people?

It is important to convey a deep sense of value to every person you encounter. Even if a person hasn't been wanted by anyone else on this earth, that person is deeply and eternally wanted by God.

To what extent do we draw spiritual strength from others who affirm us as *beloved* by God?

LESSON #2

JESUS CALLED ORDINARY PEOPLE TO FOLLOW HIM

Awe: a feeling of amazement,
coupled with the utmost respect,
at the presence of, or acknowledgment of,
one who has tremendous significance or power

B
Bible Focus

> So it was, as the multitude pressed about Him to hear the
> word of God, that He stood by the Lake of Gennesaret, and
> saw two boats standing by the lake; but the fishermen had
> gone from them and were washing their nets. Then He got into
> one of the boats, which was Simon's, and asked him to put out
> a little from the land. And He sat down and taught the multi-
> tudes from the boat.
>
> When He had stopped speaking, He said to Simon, "Launch
> out into the deep and let down your nets for a catch."
>
> But Simon answered and said to Him, "Master, we have
> toiled all night and caught nothing; nevertheless at Your word
> I will let down the net." And when they had done this, they
> caught a great number of fish, and their net was breaking. So
> they signaled to their partners in the other boat to come and
> help them. And they came and filled both the boats, so that
> they began to sink. When Simon Peter saw it, he fell down at
> Jesus' knees, saying, "Depart from me, for I am a sinful man,
> O Lord!"
>
> For he and all who were with him were astonished at the
> catch of fish which they had taken; and so also were James
> and John, the sons of Zebedee, who were partners with Simon.
> And Jesus said to Simon, "Do not be afraid. From now on you
> will catch men." So when they had brought their boats to land,
> they forsook all and followed Him (Luke 5:1–11).

Fishing was the predominant industry for the towns surrounding the Sea
of Galilee. Historians have estimated as many as two thousand boats fished
the sea during the time of Jesus. Even though the sea was teeming with fish,
not every day was a good day for fishing. In the account above, Simon Peter,
who was in the fishing business with his brother Andrew and partners James
and John, had fished all night and caught nothing. They were washing their
nets and hanging them up to dry when Jesus approached them and asked for
the use of their boat. The crowds had pressed Jesus to the water's edge and
for the people to see and hear Him clearly, He needed their boat as a plat-
form from which to speak. Simon and the others had heard Jesus and already
had some degree of relationship with Him. They quickly agreed to His
request.

After Jesus had given His teaching and dismissed the crowd, He told His
fishermen friends to row back out into the sea to the deep waters—which

can range from 80 to 160 feet in depth in the Sea of Galilee—and to let down their nets for a catch. Simon, an experienced and successful fisherman, knew this defied all fishing wisdom. Fishermen fished the sea at night so the fish could not see the shadow of the nets, and most of the fish were caught at fairly shallow depths. Simon agreed to do what Jesus said, even though he didn't expect a catch.

The fish hit the nets in such numbers that the boats Peter, James, and John were manning were filled to overflowing with what Luke described as a net-breaking, boat-sinking load of fish. Peter knew he had experienced a miracle, and he felt deeply humbled. When Peter said, "Depart from me, for I am a sinful man, O Lord!" (Luke 5:8), he was not sending Jesus away, but rather, was admitting that he felt totally unworthy of having a relationship with Jesus. He and the others with him were overwhelmed with awe. Their awe was so great it apparently paralyzed them, at least temporarily—they did not know what to say or do in the face of Jesus' great power and authority.

Jesus replied, "Do not be afraid" (Luke 5:10). In other words, "Don't be paralyzed into inaction." He then called them to great action, to become fishers of men!

These common fishermen beached their boats, left behind everything they knew as a career, and followed Jesus.

Four men with virtually no social or political standing, very little formal education, and apparently no strong ties to another rabbi or synagogue, left everything they knew and followed someone they barely knew. Why? Because Jesus had changed *everything* about the way they looked at their world.

Jesus could fashion things that were of little relevance into great blessings.

Jesus could create out of nothing exactly what was necessary.

Jesus could speak in the face of need and create abundance.

Jesus had not only found fish, but He filled their boats with a catch they had never experienced before. Now He was offering to fill their lives with a purpose and mission that was greater than anything they had ever dreamed.

That's what Jesus does today. He speaks into the ordinariness of our life and calls us to do three things:

First, give what we have for His use in spreading the gospel and building His kingdom on this earth.

Second, obey Him in whatever He calls or directs us to do—regardless of whether or not it makes sense to us or if it goes against culture, or custom.

Third, see the greatest challenge in life as winning souls and making disciples.

Very few great preachers have come from *great* families. Very few saints through history came from backgrounds of wealth or prestige. Christianity is not about who *we* are—it's about who we belong to and what He wants to do through and in us.

It is not about our ideas or opinions, but about what He commands in His infinite wisdom.

It is not about what we can accomplish in our own strength and ability, but about what He empowers and equips us to do by His Spirit.

Have you caught anything of real value lately?

A
Application for Today

The baby boy was literally found lying on a trash heap. The person who rescued the little boy from certain death took him to an orphanage where he was fed and clothed, taught to read and write, and told about Jesus.

The little boy learned to fish as he grew up. One of his favorite stories was about Jesus calling Peter, James, and John to become fishers of men. A lake was close to the orphanage, and when the boy reached the age of seven, he was allowed to go to the lake after his chores and homework were done. He would sit and fish there for hours—or at least until the supper bell rang. He didn't have a fancy pole, line, or bait—but he caught a good number of fish, which helped the orphanage leaders feed the children.

One day the little boy told the orphanage leaders, "I'd like a dad and mom." The leaders smiled and said, "All the children would like that. There just aren't enough moms and dads to go around."

The little boy refused to be discouraged. He said, "I'm going to ask Jesus for a dad and mom." Every few weeks he'd go to the orphanage leaders and ask, "Have you found a dad and mom for me?" The leaders tried to help him be realistic about his chances of being adopted, and to divert his attention to other matters, but the little boy remained singular in his focus. He'd always say as he walked away, "Jesus knows where they are, just like He knows where the fish are."

One day when he was about nine years old, the young boy went to the lake late one afternoon and saw an older boy sitting at the spot where he normally fished. The older boy said, "Are you from around here?" The orphan boy replied, "Yeah. I usually fish where you're sitting. But I can sit on this log over here." The two boys began to talk softly as they fished.

"You got any brothers or sisters?" the older boy asked.

"No," the orphan boy said.

"I don't either," the older boy said. "I keep asking my dad and mom for a brother but they just smile and don't say anything."

"I could be your brother," the orphan boy offered.

"Really?"

"Yeah. I've been looking for a dad and mom. If you'd be willing to share your dad and mom with me, I'd be willing to be your brother."

You can guess the rest of the story.

Years later, both boys had grown to become prominent men in their community. They ran a business together, served in the same church together, and lived in the same neighborhood. Everyone who saw them working or worshiping together could tell they really enjoyed each other's company. A reporter for the local newspaper one day asked the men how they had developed such a good friendship as brothers. He learned in the process one of the men was adopted. The reporter asked, "How did that come about?"

The adopted son smiled at his older brother and then replied to the reporter, "Oh, we were just fishing for each other."

Is there someone today you are *fishing for* in God's kingdom? Is there someone specifically whom you desire to see come to Christ? If not, why not? If so, what are you doing to *catch* that person for the Lord?

S
Supplementary Scriptures to Consider

Those Jews who collected taxes on Rome's behalf were greatly despised by their fellow Jews. Even so, Jesus *called* a tax collector named Levi—we know him as the writer of the Gospel of Matthew—to follow Him as a close disciple:

> After these things He went out and saw a tax collector named Levi, sitting at the tax office. And He said to him, "Follow Me." So he left all, rose up, and followed Him.
>
> Then Levi gave Him a great feast in his own house. And there were a great number of tax collectors and others who sat down with them. And their scribes and the Pharisees complained against His disciples, saying, "Why do you eat and drink with tax collectors and sinners?"
>
> Jesus answered and said to them, "Those who are well have no need of a physician, but those who are sick. I have not come to call the righteous, but sinners, to repentance" (Luke 5:27–32).

• What did Jesus mean when He said, *"Those who are well have no need of a physician, but those who are sick"*? Why is it critically important for people to recognize and confess their own sinfulness? How can guilt make us keenly aware of our need for forgiveness?

• Those who think they are perfect see no reason to change anything in their lives. To repent is to change—to turn away from something a person knows is contrary to God's best and to turn toward God in obedience. In what ways has the Lord called you to repent?

Jesus was completely dependent on God the Father for direction in His earthly life and ministry, including His choice of apostles—the ones He could entrust with His message and reputation:

> Now it came to pass in those days that He went out to the mountain to pray, and continued all night in prayer to God. And when it was day, He called His disciples to Himself; and from them He chose twelve whom He also named apostles: Simon, whom He also named Peter, and Andrew his brother; James and John; Philip and Bartholomew; Matthew and Thomas; James the son of Alphaeus, and Simon called the Zealot; Judas the son of James, and Judas Iscariot who also became a traitor (Luke 6:12–16).

- None of the men Jesus chose were famous, rich, or held spiritual or political office. Yet through them Christ changed the world. Do you believe the Lord still wants to change the world today? Are you willing to be one that He uses to do it?

- Why is it important to pray prior to any significant decision you make? Do you understand the importance of praying especially about your employees, business partners, or the people for whom you work?

- In what ways have you experienced guidance from the Lord through prayer? Can you cite an example in your life when you knew with certainty the Lord was speaking to you about what to do, and with whom?

Jesus knew God does not look at outward qualifications or personality in choosing people for leadership. The example of the prophet and high priest Samuel anointing David to be king was a story every Jew knew:

> So Samuel did what the LORD said, and went to Bethlehem. And the elders of the town trembled at his coming, and said, "Do you come peaceably?"
>
> And he said, "Peaceably; I have come to sacrifice to the LORD. Sanctify yourselves, and come with me to the sacrifice." Then he consecrated Jesse and his sons, and invited them to the sacrifice.
>
> So it was, when they came, that he looked at Eliab and said, "Surely the LORD's anointed is before Him!"
>
> But the LORD said to Samuel, "Do not look at his appearance or at his physical stature, because I have refused him. For the LORD does not see as man sees; for man looks at the outward appearance, but the LORD looks at the heart.". . .
>
> And Samuel said to Jesse, "Are all the young men here?" Then he said, "There remains yet the youngest, and there he is, keeping the sheep."
>
> And Samuel said to Jesse, "Send and bring him. For we will not sit down till he comes here." So he sent and brought him in. Now he was ruddy, with bright eyes, and good-looking. And the LORD said, "Arise, anoint him; for this is the one!" Then Samuel took the horn of oil and anointed him in the midst of his brothers, and the Spirit of the LORD came upon David from that day forward (1 Samuel 16:4–7, 11–13).

• Reflect on the statement: *"The Lord looks at the heart."* (1 Samuel 16:7). What specifically do you believe the Lord is looking for in a person's heart? Are these qualities inborn or learned? What does it mean to you to have a *heart for God*?

- Many people today seem preoccupied with outward appearances. Most products are sold on the basis of eye appeal more than any other factor. How important is outward appearance to you? Even though God looks at the heart, the Bible tells us that David was *"ruddy, with bright eyes, and good-looking"* (1 Samuel 16:12). Was this in David's favor or was David selected despite his appearance?

- Have you ever been chosen for something on the basis of outer qualities? Have you ever been chosen for something on the basis of your character traits? Which example of being *chosen* do you value the most?

I
Introspection and Implications

1. Have you ever found yourself in a position in which you felt fear about the near presence of God? Why? What did you do?

2. How does having awe of God differ from being afraid of Him?

3. Do you feel unworthy of what God has done for you, in you, or through you? Why? Is it good to feel unworthy?

4. How do humility and low self-esteem differ?

5. How challenging would it be for you to hear the Lord say, "Follow Me" and know He was asking you to give up virtually everything in your life to do His bidding?

6. What might be your *boat*—the object or entity that God may be asking you to lend to Him so He might use it to extend His kingdom?

C
Communicating the Good News

Jesus taught:

> "So the last will be first, and the first last. For many are called, but few chosen" (Matthew 20:16).

Can you cite an example of someone you know who seems to embody the truth of Jesus' teaching?

Not every person is chosen for leadership within the church or the kingdom of God, but everyone is chosen to follow Christ. Does this fact encourage or discourage you?

The Lord desires *every* person to accept Jesus as Savior and follow Him as Lord, but many people do not heed His call to their hearts. Why do you think relatively few people choose what God desires for their lives? How does this fact challenge you in your soul-winning efforts?

LESSON #3

JESUS HEALS AND DELIVERS ALL WHO COME TO HIM

*Compassion: an active move toward others
with a desire to eliminate or ease their suffering*

B
Bible Focus

> Now He rose from the synagogue and entered Simon's
> house. But Simon's wife's mother was sick with a high fever,
> and they made request of Him concerning her. So He stood
> over her and rebuked the fever, and it left her. And immedi-
> ately she arose and served them.
>
> When the sun was setting, all those who had any that were
> sick with various diseases brought them to Him; and He laid
> His hands on every one of them and healed them. And demons
> also came out of many, crying out and saying, "You are the
> Christ, the Son of God!"
>
> And He, rebuking them, did not allow them to speak for
> they knew that He was the Christ.
>
> Now when it was day, He departed, and went into a de-
> serted place. And the crowd sought Him and came to Him,
> and tried to keep Him from leaving them; but He said to them,
> "I must preach the kingdom of God to the other cities also,
> because for this purpose I have been sent." And He was
> preaching in the synagogues of Galilee" (Luke 4:38–44).

> And He came down with them and stood on a level place
> with a crowd of His disciples and a great multitude of people
> from all Judea and Jerusalem, and from the seacoast of Tyre
> and Sidon, who came to hear Him and be healed of their
> diseases, as well as those who were tormented with unclean
> spirits. And they were healed. And the whole multitude sought
> to touch Him, for power went out of Him and healed them all
> (Luke 6:17–19).

The Gospels do not present a single incident in which Jesus failed to heal
a sick person, or a person tormented with unclean spirits when a request for
healing or deliverance was made. Four things about the ministry of Jesus
stand out with great clarity as one reads the Gospels as a whole, and especially the Gospel of Luke.

First, the wellspring of Jesus' spiritual power was directly linked to
prayer. Jesus is described in numerous places in the Gospels as spending
significant time alone with His heavenly Father. It was in prayer and com-
munion with His Father that Jesus was refreshed and renewed after what had
to have been physically exhausting hours of giving. Both teaching and

healing people take tremendous amounts of physical, emotional, mental, and spiritual energy and strength.

It was in prayer Jesus knew clearly what to teach, to whom, at what time, and for what purpose.

It was in prayer Jesus was reassured, empowered, and guided how to do all He did.

It was in prayer Jesus' heart was filled to overflowing with compassion.

Do we expect the Lord to do these things for us in our prayer times?

Second, the miracles of Jesus follow behind in the wake of His preaching and teaching ministry. The first priority is on preaching and teaching. Why? Because it is the truth of God, taught and preached, that inspires faith. The apostle Paul made this point very clear in writing to the Romans: "Faith comes by hearing, and hearing by the word of God" (Romans 10:17).

Third, in the vast majority of cases recorded in the Gospels, Jesus was *asked* to heal. People brought their loved ones to Jesus, or Jesus to their loved ones. They sought Him out so He might lay His hands on them, or so they might reach out and touch Him. They were *expecting* to be healed, and they were. Faith is a foundational factor in everything we receive from the Lord. James wrote: "Let him ask in faith, with no doubting, for he who doubts is like a wave of the sea driven and tossed by the wind. For let not that man suppose that he will receive anything from the Lord; he is a double-minded man, unstable in all his ways" (James 1:6–7). This does not mean an individual needed to have faith to be healed—often it was the faith of others that resulted in healing. Sometimes it was the unlimited and perfect faith of Christ alone that manifested the faith.

Fourth, no disease or ailment was too difficult for Jesus to heal. His Word and His touch were more powerful than any disease, ailment, or evil spirit. He had command over *all* things.

What is the message to us as His followers?

We are called to be a people of prayer. It is in prayer we encounter the living Lord and He strengthens us, and we grow in relationship with Him. It is in prayer His Spirit confirms to our hearts that what we have read in the Bible is true, and we receive specific direction and encouragement from the Lord.

We are called to be a people of the Word. We are not only to know the Scriptures, but to speak the truth of the Scriptures to others.

We are called to be people of faith. We are to trust God with utter abandon, believing He can do all things according to His methods, His timing, and always for His glory.

We are called to be a people who regard *nothing* as impossible with God. If Christ be for us, who can be against us. We can do all things in His strength. (See Romans 8:31 and Philippians 4:13.)

A
Application for Today

Poll-taking statisticians have determined in recent years that one in four dollars in the economies of western nations is spent on health care. Health care is big business with many facets. Health is a concern of all people, not just those who are sick. In all likelihood, it was a major concern at the time of Jesus, although fewer monetary resources were involved.

There are dozens of questions we might ask about our faith and how it relates to health and sickness.

Where do *you* go for healing? When you are sick, to whom do you turn? Some go to a family physician. Some to neighborhood clinic or to a walk-in patient center at a hospital. Some just go to the medicine cabinet in the bathroom.

We live in a world that seems to have dozens of options for health care. Do you ever go *first* to someone who can pray for you to be healed? Do you have faith to believe that prayer really works in healing physical sickness? How about emotional and mental illness?

Where do you turn when you want to know more about sickness and health?

Information about diseases and ailments and their cures is readily available on the Internet and in a wide variety of other media formats. Do you ever think of turning to God's Word for information about sickness and health? Why or why not?

How much pain or distress do you have to feel before you seek help in overcoming a sickness or injury? Some people go quickly for health care the minute they experience the slightest symptom of illness. Some people wait until a disease is advanced before they seek help. How quick are you to ask God to heal you—when you first feel a cold coming on, or do you wait until you receive a dire diagnosis?

What role does faith play in a world with advanced scientific medicine?

Is faith involved when a person takes a pill and anticipates a headache will go away? Is faith involved when a person goes to a doctor and follows the doctor's advice, believing the advice will lead to a cure?

What impact does prayer have on preventing illness? Reversing illness? Helping an injury heal faster?

Is there any illness you believe is too difficult for Jesus to heal?

S
Supplementary Scriptures to Consider

Jesus was certainly familiar with the words of the great prophets of Israel, including the prophet Zechariah:

> Then the word of the LORD came to Zechariah, saying,
> "Thus says the LORD of hosts:
> 'Execute true justice,
> Show mercy and compassion
> Everyone to his brother" (Zechariah 7:8–9).

We often think in terms of *true justice* as delivering punishment to those who do wrong. How does the Lord perceive *true justice* in this passage? In what ways does praying for the healing and deliverance of others express mercy and compassion? In what ways do acts of compassion break a cycle of vengeance? In what ways do acts of mercy and compassion set injustices right?

When John the Baptist was imprisoned, he sent messengers to confirm that Jesus was, indeed, the Messiah. John knew if Jesus was the Christ, his work was essentially over and he could face death in peace.

> When the men had come to Him, they said, "John the Baptist has sent us to You, saying, 'Are You the Coming One, or do we look for another?'" And that very hour He cured many of infirmities, afflictions, and evil spirits; and to many blind He gave sight.
> Jesus answered and said to them, "Go and tell John the things you have seen and heard: that the blind see, the lame walk, the lepers are cleansed, the deaf hear, the dead are raised, the poor have the gospel preached to them. And blessed is he who is not offended because of Me" (Luke 7:20–23).

• Jesus answered those sent from John with deeds, and then gave a message for them to take back to John. How important is it for each of us to validate what we say about Jesus with our deeds?

• How do you respond to those who place an emphasis on faith alone, and do very little to help others in practical ways? How do you respond to those who are full of good works, but never mention the name of Jesus? What is the balance you desire for your own life?

Jesus did not need to be physically present to heal:

> Now when He concluded all His sayings in the hearing of the people, He entered Capernaum. And a certain centurion's servant, who was dear to him, was sick and ready to die. So when he heard about Jesus, he sent elders of the Jews to Him, pleading with Him to come and heal his servant. And when they came to Jesus, they begged Him earnestly, saying that the one for whom He should do this was deserving, "for he loves our nation, and has built us a synagogue."
> Then Jesus went with them. And when He was already not far from the house, the centurion sent friends to Him, saying to Him, "Lord, do not trouble Yourself, for I am not worthy

that You should enter under my roof. Therefore I did not even think myself worthy to come to You. But say the word, and my servant will be healed. For I also am a man placed under authority, having soldiers under me. And I say to one, 'Go,' and he goes; and to another, 'Come,' and he comes; and to my servant, 'Do this,' and he does it."

When Jesus heard these things, He marveled at him, and turned around and said to the crowd that followed Him, "I say to you, I have not found such great faith, not even in Israel!" And those who were sent, returning to the house, found the servant well who had been sick" (Luke 7:1–10).

• As you pray for your loved ones, in what ways does this account in the Gospels encourage you as a person who isn't in the immediate presence of Jesus?

• Based on what you know about the totality of Jesus' message and healing ministry, do you believe He went to the centurion's home because He was begged earnestly, because the man was apparently a *good person*, or because He perceived God's opportunity in the situation? What is the role of asking God to act on behalf of another person? Is one person ever more worthy than another to experience God's healing power?

- Jesus applauded this man's faith. What do you believe Jesus would say about your faith? The faith level in your church? How important is it to recognize that every person has a measure of faith with which to believe? What might we do to activate our faith in greater ways?

I
Introspection and Implications

1. Has anyone ever prayed for your healing? How did you respond? What happened?

2. Have you ever prayed for another person to be healed? How did you pray? What happened?

3. The Bible says in James 4:2, "You do not have because you do not ask." What is the role of asking God for something you know He's already aware you need?

4. Do you ever struggle in believing Jesus has absolute power over all manner of sickness and disease? How might this belief-struggle or faith-crisis impact the way in which you pray?

5. In what ways does praying with another person boost your own faith to believe for God's best?

6. Do you ever find it easier to pray for another person than to pray for yourself? Why might that be the case?

C
Communicating the Good News

How do miracles, signs, and wonders attract those who don't know Jesus?

How do miracles, signs, and wonders encourage those who do know Jesus as Savior?

In what ways do we dismiss or discount the value of miracles, signs, and wonders in evangelism of the lost?

In what ways are we frightened of miracles, signs, and wonders?

How can we keep ourselves from being preoccupied with miracles, signs, and wonders to the point that we lose sight of the simplicity, purity, and power of the gospel message?

In what ways should miracles, signs, and wonders be regarded as a normal extension and aftermath of our praying and preaching?

LESSON #4

JESUS HAS COMPASSION ON SINNERS AND OUTCASTS

*Faith: the ability to believe
for ultimate good*

B
Bible Focus

> *Then one of the Pharisees asked Him to eat with him. And He went to the Pharisee's house, and sat down to eat. And behold, a woman in the city who was a sinner, when she knew that Jesus sat at the table in the Pharisee's house, brought an alabaster flask of fragrant oil, and stood at His feet behind Him weeping; and she began to wash His feet with her tears, and wiped them with the hair of her head; and she kissed His feet and anointed them with the fragrant oil. Now when the Pharisee who had invited Him saw this, he spoke to himself, saying, "This Man, if He were a prophet, would know who and what manner of woman this is who is touching Him, for she is a sinner."*
>
> *And Jesus answered and said to him, "Simon, I have something to say to you."*
>
> *So he said, "Teacher, say it."*
>
> *"There was a certain creditor who had two debtors. One owed five hundred denarii, and the other fifty. And when they had nothing with which to repay, he freely forgave them both. Tell Me, therefore, which of them will love him more?"*
>
> *Simon answered and said, "I suppose the one whom he forgave more."*
>
> *And He said to him, "You have rightly judged." Then He turned to the woman and said to Simon, "Do you see this woman? I entered your house; you gave Me no water for My feet, but she has washed My feet with her tears and wiped them with the hair of her head. You gave Me no kiss, but this woman has not ceased to kiss My feet since the time I came in. You did not anoint My head with oil, but this woman has anointed My feet with fragrant oil. Therefore I say to you, her sins, which are many, are forgiven, for she loved much. But to whom little is forgiven, the same loves little."*
>
> *Then He said to her, "Your sins are forgiven."*
>
> *And those who sat at the table with Him began to say to themselves, "Who is this who even forgives sins?"*
>
> *Then He said to the woman, "Your faith has saved you. Go in peace" (Luke 7:36–50).*

The Jewish world was very concerned with what was *clean* and *unclean*. The Law of Moses identified a wide variety of substances and behaviors that could render a person *unclean*, from touching a dead animal to having an open sore. Centuries of man-made laws had expanded the definition of *unclean* to include virtually anything deemed morally or spiritually suspect.

The Gentile world as a whole—both then and now—has also differentiated between good and bad, right and wrong. In human terms, we tend to classify human beings as *good* people or *bad* people, behaviors as *appropriate* or *inappropriate*, and statements as being socially or politically *correct* or *incorrect*.

The Jews believed a *clean* person could become polluted by an *unclean* person, and the resulting consequence was to be ostracized from the greater society for a period of time and undergo specified purification rituals. Those who did not seek to avoid contact with *unclean* people were subject to ridicule. The Gentile world also held similar opinions, although expressed differently. Even today, we hear phrases such as "one bad apple can spoil the whole barrel."

In the Bible passage above, a Pharisee asked Jesus to come to dinner. Jesus accepted the invitation. The custom of the time was for a person inviting a guest—and especially a guest with a degree of fame—to leave the gate to his courtyard open so others who wanted to participate in a time of fellowship before or after the meal might have contact with the guest. The host, of course, benefited from this by being perceived as a generous and hospitable person. The guest had an opportunity to meet more people, and the townspeople had opportunity to ask questions or engage in conversation with notable teachers or people of accomplishment.

It was also customary at that time for all people to take off their sandals before sitting down to a meal. The tables were usually very low and people sat on cushions as they ate. A good host generally provided his guests with two things: water to wash the feet (and when possible, a servant to do the washing), and some sort of fragrance for soothing and refreshing both skin and hair. The Pharisee in the incident above did neither for Jesus.

One of the people who wandered into the Pharisee's courtyard that day was a prostitute. She fell at Jesus' feet and washed His feet with her tears and anointed His feet with expensive fragrance. An *unclean* woman had touched Jesus, and those present were acutely aware of this breach of etiquette. The people were appalled that Jesus *allowed* it to happen and concluded He couldn't tell what kind of woman she was; therefore, according to their faulty line of thinking, He must be a man with no spiritual discernment and thus, be a false prophet.

Jesus made it very clear in His parable: A person's status as *unclean* or *sinner* does not disqualify that person from God's forgiveness or mercy. In truth, God loved all of us while we were sinners. He extended mercy and forgiveness to every one of us while we were still in an *unclean* or *sinful* state. Furthermore, nothing a person does or doesn't do qualifies him or her for salvation, other than an expression of repentance or sorrow for sin and a desire for God.

This woman was not forgiven that day because she washed Jesus' feet with her tears and applied expensive ointment to His feet. She was forgiven because she loved Him, desired to be in relationship with God, and deeply grieved her sin.

Whom do we consider to be *unclean* today? Whom would we prefer *not* come into our church services or seek to join our church? Whom do we avoid? Whom do we consider to be beyond deserving redemption?

To what extent do we require people to *clean up their act* before they come to God?

To what degree do we extend greater mercy to people we perceive as being *good folk* with good hearts and lesser mercy to those we perceive as being hard-core sinners with dark hearts?

In what ways do we require people to engage in behaviors of our liking before we truly accept them?

If you had been in the room with Jesus, the Pharisee host, and this woman, what would you have said or done?

A
Application for Today

He sat down on the curb outside the church entrance and watched several dozen well-dressed people file into the building. A brown sack next to him appeared to be wrapped around what looked like a liquor bottle. He was dressed in castaway clothing and obviously hadn't shaved in several days.

No one said anything to him. No one invited him to come into the church.

As he sat on the curb he heard several people say something *about* him to designated greeter at the front door. They muttered, "Should we ask him to move?", "I hope his sitting there doesn't give a bad impression to a first-time visitor," and "What are you going to do if he tries to come in?"

One person asked the greeter, "Does the new pastor know about this guy?" The greeter replied, "I haven't seen the new pastor yet." The first person responded, "You mean the new preacher isn't here yet?" The greeter looked at his watch and said, "No. I'm getting a little concerned. The music minister has been out here twice asking if he's arrived. Something must have happened."

A few minutes later the church door was closed and music played from the church organ. The congregation began to sing. As the people sat down after the opening hymn, they were startled to hear the back door of the church open and to see the curbside bum walk boldly down the aisle. He walked all the way to the front, climbed the stairs, and then positioned himself behind the lectern. The church people were frantic, their eyes darting to one another with wide-eyed expressions that seemed to ask, "What's going on? What's going to happen?"

The unkempt man held up his hands, smiled broadly, and said in a booming voice, "Good morning. I'm your new pastor."

The crowd gasped.

The preacher then lowered his voice and said, "We have work to do."

If you had been a member of that church walking into the building that Sunday morning, what would you have done about the man sitting on the curb? Would you have said anything *to* him? *About* him?

If you had been a church member sitting in the pew as the man walked up the aisle, would you have done anything?

What would go through your mind if you had been a member of that church hearing the new pastor introduce himself?

S
Supplementary Scriptures to Consider

Many people look for justification for failing to tell someone about Jesus, or for failing to do the right thing:

> And behold, a certain lawyer stood up and tested Him, saying, "Teacher, what shall I do to inherit eternal life?"
>
> He said to him, "What is written in the law? What is your reading of it?"
>
> So he answered and said, "'You shall love the LORD your God with all your heart, with all your soul, with all your strength, and with all your mind,' and 'your neighbor as yourself.'"
>
> And He said to him, "You have answered rightly; do this and you will live."
>
> But he, wanting to justify himself, said to Jesus, "And who is my neighbor?"
>
> Then Jesus answered and said: "A certain man went down from Jerusalem to Jericho, and fell among thieves, who stripped him of his clothing, wounded him, and departed, leaving him half dead. Now by chance a certain priest came down that road. And when he saw him, he passed by on the other side. Likewise a Levite, when he arrived at the place, came and looked, and passed by on the other side. But a certain Samaritan, as he journeyed, came where he was. And when he saw him, he had compassion. So he went to him

and bandaged his wounds, pouring on oil and wine; and he
set him on his own animal, brought him to an inn, and took
care of him. On the next day, when he departed, he took out
two denarii, gave them to the innkeeper, and said to him,
'Take care of him; and whatever more you spend, when I
come again, I will repay you.' So which of these three do
you think was neighbor to him who fell among the thieves?"

And he said, "He who has showed mercy on him."

Then Jesus said to him, "Go and do likewise" (Luke
10:25–37).

• What is the better alternative to giving excuses and self-justification?

• Why do you believe we all want God's mercy, but we are reluctant to
show God's mercy to others?

• The priest and Levite in this story may have had what they perceived to
be good excuses for ignoring this man. They may have thought he was
dead, they may have been concerned they needed to remain ceremonially clean to fulfill their duties in the temple, or they may have been
afraid the man was faking his injuries and was functioning as a decoy

for an ambush. Do any such excuses matter? What excuses do we make for not doing more to alleviate suffering in the world?

- What does it mean to show mercy (compassion on the undeserving) to another person? Is there a difference between human mercy and God's mercy? How do we show *God's* mercy to others? In what ways is showing mercy more potent than telling about God's mercy?

I
Introspection and Implications

1. Would you have knelt to wash Jesus' feet with your tears as the woman did in Luke 7:36–50? If not, what would have kept you from doing this?

2. Do you have an *alabaster box* of something precious the Lord wants you to pour out on Him? How would you do that?

3. Can you think of anyone beyond God's mercy? Someone unworthy to be forgiven?

4. Can a person ever be sorrowful enough for their sins?

5. Can a person ever be thankful enough for their salvation?

C
Communicating the Good News

Mercy is God *not* giving us what we deserve. *Grace* is God giving us far more than we deserve. Every Christian today is the recipient of mercy (not being punished for our sin) and grace (being extended salvation and spiritual gifts):

> But God, who is rich in mercy, because of His great love
> with which He loved us, even when we were dead in tres-
> passes, made us alive together with Christ (by grace you
> have been saved), and raised us up together, and made us sit
> together in the heavenly places in Christ Jesus, that in the
> ages to come He might show the exceeding riches of His
> grace in His kindness toward us in Christ Jesus. For by grace
> you have been saved through faith, and that not of your-
> selves; it is the gift of God, not of works, lest anyone should
> boast. For we are His workmanship, created in Christ Jesus
> for good works, which God prepared beforehand that we
> should walk in them" (Ephesians 2:4–10).

Why is it important to extend words of mercy and grace to those who haven't received Jesus as their Savior?

Why is it important to display merciful deeds to those who don't know Jesus as Savior?

In what ways might we encourage one another as believers to open ourselves more fully to God's grace?

LESSON #5

JESUS EMPHASIZES LOVE AND EXTENDS FORGIVENESS TO ALL

Love: to give with generosity what will bless another person

Forgiveness: to release a person from punishment for a mistake or wrongdoing; to release a person from one's hatred

B
Bible Focus

> *Then He lifted up His eyes toward His disciples and said. . . .*
>
> *"But I say to you who hear: Love your enemies, do good to those who hate you, bless those who curse you, and pray for those who spitefully use you. To him who strikes you on the one cheek, offer the other also. And from him who takes away your cloak, do not withhold your tunic either. Give to everyone who asks of you. And from him who takes away your goods do not ask them back. And just as you want men to do to you, you also do to them likewise.*
>
> *"But if you love those who love you, what credit is that to you? For even sinners love those who love them. And if you do good to those who do good to you, what credit is that to you? For even sinners do the same. And if you lend to those from whom you hope to receive back, what credit is that to you? For even sinners lend to sinners to receive as much back. But love your enemies, do good, and lend, hoping for nothing in return; and your reward will be great, and you will be sons of the Most High. For He is kind to the unthankful and evil. Therefore be merciful, just as your Father also is merciful.*
>
> *"Judge not, and you shall not be judged. Condemn not, and you shall not be condemned. Forgive, and you will be forgiven. Give, and it will be given to you: good measure, pressed down, shaken together, and running over will be put into your bosom. For with the same measure that you use, it will be measured back to you"* (Luke 6:20, 27–38).

A common phrase in our world today says, "What goes around, comes around." This general law of reciprocity is basic to most human cultures. However, it is not what is at the core of Jesus' teaching in the Gospels.

"What goes around, comes around" assumes human behavior sparks a cycle of human behavior, so what Person 'A' does to another human being will eventually be what Person 'A' receives from another human being— perhaps not the same human being, but ultimately, from a human source. In other words, if you are unfaithful to or hurt a person, eventually, someone will be unfaithful to you or hurt you.

Jesus taught, in contrast, that what we do brings a response from *God* that may be very different than the normal response from people—and it is the response from God that counts.

The law of reciprocity would say, "If a person hits you, hit them back."

"If a person steals from you steal back or take them to court!" "If a person condemns you to others, undermine their slander and take them down with you."

Jesus said, "If a person hits you, let him hit you again." "If a person steals from you, give him something additional of value." "If a person condemns you, speak well of them." In the end, God will see and will act.

How difficult it is for most of us to do things Jesus' way!

Furthermore, human logic says we are capable of judging others, of deciding whether a person is good or bad, innocent or guilty. We are also capable of issuing a fair punishment; at a minimum, declaring a person to be unworthy of receiving something good.

Jesus taught we are *not* to judge others, in part because we cannot know everything about another person, all the factors involved in any situation of their life, or the enormity of God's love or the nature of God's plan for the person. We are *not* capable of just condemnation because we are incapable of reading motives, potential, or the human heart. Judgment and punishment-rendering related to personhood belong solely to God.

The human law of reciprocity sets up a cycle of vengeance and retaliation that never ends. Pain is multiplied into more pain. Anger is allowed to seethe, bitterness takes root and grows, and hatred flares into violence and abuse. Many cultures have multiple generations of hurt, pain, and unforgiveness against other ethnic groups that continue to be passed on to succeeding generations still today.

Jesus' teachings advocate a way to stop a cycle of vengeance. Forgiveness sets into motion a cycle of generous giving, which results in generous reward *from God*. God, who has all forces and influence at His command, can reward us through people in ways we could never engineer! God is the only true judge of any person, and He is capable of bringing about justice on our behalf in ways we could never imagine. Forgiveness sets us free from man-made standards of goodness and man-made customs and allows us to pursue what God says is acceptable, desirable, and eternally beneficial. In the end, God rewards us as only He can. His rewards are far beyond anything a human being can bestow. God's best is *the* best.

A
Application for Today

Joey hit Billy and gave him a bruise on his arm.

Billy hit Joey back, and gave him a black eye.

Joey's sister Geraldine saw the black eye and walloped Billy, which brought Billy's older brother Greg into the fray. He took on both Joey and Geraldine and left them in pain and tears.

Joey and Geraldine went running to their mom, who called Billy's mom, who promptly stood by her children. Billy's mom felt insulted and before nightfall Billy's dad had gone over to Joey's house and verbally abusing the entire family on their front porch.

Neighbors who had witnessed the growing fight took sides. Before long, the town was pretty much evenly split. No one could remember *why* Joey hit Billy. It didn't matter. Insults and tears and angry words had flown about fast and furiously, and there was plenty of reason to find fault all around.

The relatives of those in the town eventually heard about the growing feud, and they weighed in with their opinions. Things began to take on cultural, racial, and even political overtones. Some attacks were open—of the hit-and-run variety. Others took place under the cover of night.

Then someone realized most of those on one side were of one religious persuasion and those on the other side were of another religious persuasion. Things really got ugly at that point. Now there was *real* reason to fight and win.

And so it went.

Twenty years later someone found a little note that had been written, but never sent: "Dear Billy, I was just trying to get your attention to keep you from stepping on a hornet's nest, and I punched you a little too hard. Your friend, Joey."

By the time the note was discovered, no one cared. Too many people had been injured, too much property damaged, and too many angry words spoken for peace to break out.

Have you ever been involved in a cycle of vengeance?

To what degree are many ethnic groups in our world today caught up in cycles of vengeance?

What effective alternative is there other than forgiveness?

When people are screaming at one another, how might a message of forgiveness be voiced so it truly can be heard?

When people are caught up in hatred, how might a message of forgiveness be expressed in a way that it truly can be received?

When people are intent on retaliation, how might a message of forgiveness be displayed in a way that makes a real difference?

S
Supplementary Scriptures to Consider

Although God extends mercy and forgiveness to all, not everyone takes Him up on His offer:

Now when one of those who sat at the table with Him heard these things, he said to Him, "Blessed is he who shall eat bread in the kingdom of God!"

Then He said to him, "A certain man gave a great supper and invited many, and sent his servant at supper time to say to those who were invited, 'Come, for all things are now ready.' But they all with one accord began to make excuses. The first said to him, I have bought a piece of ground, and I must go and see it. I ask you to have me excused.' And another said, 'I have bought five yoke of oxen, and I am going to test them. I ask you to have me excused.' Still another said, 'I have married a wife, and therefore I cannot come.' So that servant came and reported these things to his master. Then the master of the house, being angry, said to his servant, 'Go out quickly into the streets and lanes of the city, and bring in here the poor and the maimed and the lame and the blind.' And the servant said, 'Master, it is done as you commanded, and still there is room.' Then the master said to the servant, 'Go out into the highways and hedges, and compel them to come in, that my house may be filled. For I say to you that none of those men who were invited shall taste my supper'" (Luke 14:15–24).

• What excuses have you heard people make for not accepting the forgiveness God offers through Jesus Christ? Identify several of these excuses. Respond to each one.

- In this parable of Jesus, some of the *desired* guests declined the invitation to the feast. Jesus opened the invitation to those who were considered ceremonially unclean or undesirable. In what ways do we sometimes seek out certain people to join our church, or to receive our witness, because we see them as desirable assets to the kingdom of God? In what ways do we sometimes treat the uneducated, poor, sick, or impaired as liabilities—as people requiring more from us than they can give in return?

- In this parable, the master of the feast eventually sent the servant into the *highways and hedges*, the mainstream of wicked society, including those who had "fallen off the road into the bushes." These were total strangers, even derelicts! Who would you identify today as being a total stranger to God? How might that person be reached with the gospel?

I
Introspection and Implications

1. How difficult is it for you *not* to retaliate when someone treats you badly or says unkind things about you? When are we to speak up in our own defense, and when are we to quietly take what is dished out to us?

2. Reflect on Jesus' words, *"For He is kind to the unthankful and evil"* (Luke 6:35). Can you recall a time when you showed kindness to someone who was ungrateful, abusive or who rejected your kindness?

3. What is the balance between judging *people* as good or bad and judging *behavior* as good or bad? How difficult is it to love people and hate their sin?

4. Have you ever been caught in a cycle of vengeance? What happened?

5. Reflect on these words of Jesus: "Give to everyone who asks of you" (Luke 6:30). In this day, most people receive dozens of requests for charitable contributions. How do you decide to whom to give? Is a person truly to give to *everyone* who asks for something? Is there a difference between a private request and a public request?

6. Jesus said about our giving, "For with the same measure that you use, it will be measured back to you" (Luke 6:38). Are you receiving from the Lord in generous quantity today? Do you believe what you are receiving is a reflection of the way you have been giving?

C
Communicating the Good News

To what degree is *giving* a factor in our Christian witness?

What do some of the unsaved people you know say about a person who turns the other cheek or gives to those who steal from him? Is this likely an immediate or surface response, or a deep and lasting response? How might the Holy Spirit use a Christian's generosity in forgiveness and refusal to retaliate to touch an unsaved person's heart?

Jesus taught, "Freely you have received, freely give" (Matthew 10:8). What does it mean to you to *freely* give to another person? To *freely* give the gospel?

LESSON #6

JESUS SEEKS OUT THE LOST

*Lost: unable to find your way to a place
you want to be, or something beyond
your ability to locate it or regain it*

B
Bible Focus

Then He said: "A certain man had two sons. And the younger of them said to his father, 'Father, give me the portion of goods that falls to me.' So he divided to them his livelihood. And not many days after, the younger son gathered all together, journeyed to a far country, and there wasted his possessions with prodigal living. But when he had spent all, there arose a severe famine in that land, and he began to be in want. Then he went and joined himself to a citizen of that country, and he sent him into his fields to feed swine. And he would gladly have filled his stomach with the pods that the swine ate, and no one gave him anything.

But when he came to himself, he said, 'How many of my father's hired servants have bread enough and to spare, and I perish with hunger! I will arise and go to my father, and will say to him, "Father, I have sinned against heaven and before you, and I am no longer worthy to be called your son. Make me like one of your hired servants."'

"And he arose and came to his father. But when he was still a great way off, his father saw him and had compassion, and ran and fell on his neck and kissed him. And the son said to him, 'Father, I have sinned against heaven and in your sight, and am no longer worthy to be called your son.'

"But the father said to his servants, 'Bring out the best robe and put it on him, and put a ring on his hand and sandals on his feet. And bring the fatted calf here and kill it, and let us eat and be merry; for this my son was dead and is alive again; he was lost and is found.' And they began to be merry.

"Now his older son was in the field. And as he came and drew near to the house, he heard music and dancing. So he called one of the servants and asked what these things meant. And he said to him, 'Your brother has come, and because he has received him safe and sound, your father has killed the fatted calf.'

"But he was angry and would not go in. Therefore his father came out and pleaded with him. So he answered and said to his father, 'Lo, these many years I have been serving you; I never transgressed your commandment at any time; and yet you never gave me a young goat, that I might make merry with my friends. But as soon as this son of yours came, who has devoured your livelihood with harlots, you killed the fatted calf for him.'

"And he said to him, 'Son, you are always with me, and all that I have is yours. It was right that we should make merry and be glad, for your brother was dead and is alive again, and was lost and is found'" (Luke 15:11–32).

Jesus told this story to the religious leaders of His day—people who tended to be highly critical of any person perceived to be a *sinner*. The common people of the Galilee were often called the *people of the dirt* by the Pharisees and scribes. In other words, they were regarded as being as unimportant as dust, and as unclean as possible; therefore, they were to be avoided whenever possible.

We often refer to this story as the Parable of the Prodigal Son. Some call it the Parable of the Loving Father. It might also be called the Parable of the Judgmental Older Brother.

To gain the most meaning from this parable, we need to understand something about the culture and customs of Jesus' day.

First, it was the custom for the eldest son in a family to receive double the inheritance of other sons. It was considered to be a major insult for any son to request his inheritance before the father's death. The younger son in this story not only requested his inheritance, but then left his father's home. In rebellion, he went to a *far country* and engaged in a lifestyle opposite to everything his godly father had taught him.

Second, Roman cities were established throughout the area that Rome had occupied, including the Galilee. These cities functioned according to Roman culture, not Jewish custom. They were places of sacrifice to Roman gods—cattle offered to the gods above and swine offered to the gods below. The sacrifices and resulting feasts offered to these gods produced great gluttony and debauchery, including gambling, sexual sins, and violence-producing sport. A person didn't need to travel more than fifteen or twenty miles to get to a Roman city. A Roman city, nonetheless, was as far away from God as a good Jew could get.

Third, the Jews perceived those who worked among the swine to be totally tainted by what was considered unclean. The Romans perceived the swine-keepers as those who were keepers of the sacrifices to the gods below, associated with evil powers. In our terms today, this prodigal son had fallen into the pits of sinful living, even to the depths of pagan worship.

The good news is that this young man *came to himself* and was determined to return home. His father openly and graciously received him.

Jesus said the father saw the boy when he was still *a great way off*. This was important! The boy had committed such a grievous sin against his father that he was subject to punishment by others in his town. If they saw him first, they could stone him, either killing him or prohibiting him from entering the town. It was only if the boy's own father embraced him and accepted him that the townspeople also had an obligation to accept him.

In the story, Jesus said the boy's father ran to him, embraced him, and welcomed him home. Then, he ordered the killing of an animal that was being fattened, which was generally done in anticipation of a major family religious feast. The father gave his son sandals, which indicated the son had full sonship and full permission to come and go as he desired. (Slaves at that time went barefoot.) The father gave him a signet ring, with which the boy could conduct family business. He further gave his son the privilege of wearing a special ceremonial family robe, which was a high honor at a family feast.

The older son, many think represented the religious leaders, was offended and angry his father had given such recognition and honor to his wayward younger brother. The father said to the older brother, "My honoring your brother takes nothing from you. I am valuing him, not devaluing you."

And what about us today?

We may not sink to the lowest forms of sin before we come to our senses and receive Christ Jesus as our Savior, but we are all in some degree rebellious against God before we experience His forgiveness. We are in league with the devil to some degree, knowingly or unknowingly, before we seek God's mercy.

The Father sees us when we are far from Him. He is waiting for us. He eagerly receives us when we come to Him. He shields us from destruction so He might save us from damnation. Our heavenly Father says we have the privilege of conducting spiritual business in Jesus' name, we are given a robe of righteousness that covers our sinful nature, and He gives us the means to go back out into the world and become a blessing to others instead of a curse to ourselves.

What about the way we treat those who do not know the Lord?

What about the way we accept new believers into our churches?

We are called by the Lord to rejoice at their repentance and renewal. We are called to receive them with open arms of welcome.

All of us were lost before Christ found us. We must acknowledge the tremendous truth that Christ loved us and died for us while we were sinners. We are only in a position to love Him because He first loved us.

A
Application for Today

What do you consider to be the most ungodly place in town?

Is it a place where down-and-outers gather?

Is it the local strip joint, a sleazy bar, a porn shop, a run-down motel on the edge of town?

Or, is it a place where up-and-outers can sin under the protection or secrecy of private membership? Is it a meeting place where people concoct schemes that line their pockets at the expense of the community as a whole?

Is it a part of town you've never visited, and would be afraid to visit even in daylight hours? Is it the city jail or prison?

Or, is it perhaps the house next door, where you know with certainty someone is being abused?

How do you believe Jesus feels about that place?

How do you think Jesus feels about the people who live in that house or neighborhood, go to that place, work in that place, or participate in that sin?

What do you believe can be done to shine the light of the gospel in that place? How might the light be turned on?

S
Supplementary Scriptures to Consider

In the Middle East, shepherds lead their sheep. A sheep gets lost because it fails to follow the shepherd and chooses to go its own way:

> Then all the tax collectors and sinners drew near to Him to hear Him. And the Pharisees and scribes complained, saying, "This Man receives sinners and eats with them." So He spoke this parable to them, saying:
>
> "What man of you, having a hundred sheep, if he loses one of them, does not leave the ninety-nine in the wilderness, and go after the one which is lost until he finds it? And when he has found it, he lays it on his shoulders, rejoicing. And when he comes home, he calls together his friends and neighbors, saying to them, 'Rejoice with me, for I have found my sheep which was lost!' I say to you that likewise there will be more joy in heaven over one sinner who repents than over ninety-nine just persons who need no repentance" (Luke 15:1–7).

• What might cause you to fail at times to hear Jesus' voice as He leads you? What hope does this story give you?

- In what ways do you want to go your own way, rather than follow after Jesus? What is your responsibility? What hope does this parable of Jesus give you?

- What does Jesus say is your responsibility to other people who have erred or rebelled against God?

The Jewish people had a very strong tradition of thinking of themselves as being the bride of God. (See Isaiah 61:10 and 62:5.) In Jesus' time, a married woman wore a headband with ten coins. Fewer coins indicated that she was an unmarried woman:

> "Or what woman, having ten silver coins, if she loses one coin, does not light a lamp, sweep the house, and search carefully until she finds it? And when she has found it, she calls her friends and neighbors together, saying, 'Rejoice with me, for I have found the piece which I lost!' Likewise, I say to you, there is joy in the presence of the angels of God over one sinner who repents" (Luke 15:8–10).

- In this parable, Jesus was telling the religious leaders they had lost their identity as the *bride of God* by the uncaring way they acted toward other people. How might we lose part of our identity in Christ through sheer carelessness in the way we speak and act?

• What does it mean to you to have Christian ethics? What does it mean to you to be a moral person? How important to you is your integrity? What does it mean to you to be *intentional* at all times in the way you treat other people? Is there a need for you to repent of your carelessness and recommit your life to pursuing the highest standards of integrity, morality, and godly care of others?

Those who collected taxes for Rome often padded the tax bills and skimmed off the excess for themselves. Tax collectors were despised and distrusted. For Jesus to seek out a tax collector was almost scandalous:

> Then Jesus entered and passed through Jericho. Now behold, there was a man named Zacchaeus who was a chief tax collector and he was rich. And he sought to see who Jesus was, but could not because of the crowd, for he was of short stature. So he ran ahead and climbed up into a sycamore tree to see Him, for He was going to pass that way. And when Jesus came to the place, He looked up and saw him, and said to him, "Zacchaeus, make haste and come down, for today I must stay at your house." So he made haste and came down, and received Him joyfully. But when they saw it, they all complained, saying, "He has gone to be a guest with a man who is a sinner."
>
> Then Zacchaeus stood and said to the Lord, "Look, Lord, I give half of my goods to the poor; and if I have taken anything from anyone by false accusation, I restore fourfold."
>
> And Jesus said to him, "Today salvation has come to this house, because he also is a son of Abraham; for the Son of Man has come to seek and to save that which was lost" (Luke 19:1–10).

• Jesus did not pronounce salvation on Zacchaeus *because* of his sudden vow about doing the right thing; rather, because Zacchaeus had a change of heart, admitted he had done wrong, and expressed a desire to do what was right. Confession of sin is a vital part of our receiving God's forgiveness. How often do you confess to the Lord you have sinned? In what ways is confession a prerequisite for forgiveness? How is forgiveness a prerequisite for receiving God's help in making genuine behavioral change?

• Zacchaeus not only had a change of heart, but a change of behavior. Why is it important we translate the God's forgiveness into genuine change of previously sinful behavior?

I
Introspection and Implications

1. Have you ever openly and willfully rebelled against God? What was the result?

2. Have you ever wondered if you have sinned to the degree God can no longer forgive your sin? What does the story Jesus told say to you regarding that?

3. How important is it to remain sharply aware at all times of the impact our words and actions have on others? How do our words and actions impact our own spiritual growth?

4. Reflect on this statement: "God's forgiveness does not give us license to do what we want, but rather gives us the privilege of doing what God requires." Do you agree or disagree? Why or why not?

5. How difficult is it *not* to be like the older brother in Jesus' parable about the wayward son and loving father? Why do we resent the way

some people seem to get off *free* without ever experiencing any consequence for their sin—especially their sin against *us*?

C
Communicating the Good News

It is always important to assure an unsaved person that he has *not* sinned beyond God's ability to forgive his sin. How can your own life be an example of this?

What is the balance between going where the sinner is, and inviting the sinner to come to where we are? Literally? Figuratively?

How do we best intercede in prayer for those who have gone into a *far country*?

LESSON #7

JESUS TEACHES FAITHFULNESS AND WATCHFULNESS

Faithfulness: living in a way that is consistently trustworthy and loyal, devoted and true

Watchfulness: carefully observant and alert at all times

B
Bible Focus

Now great multitudes went with Him. And He turned and said to them, "If anyone comes to Me and does not hate his father and mother, wife and children, brothers and sisters, yes, and his own life also, he cannot be My disciple. And whoever does not bear his cross and come after Me cannot be My disciple. And whoever does not bear his cross and come after Me cannot be My disciple. For which of you, intending to build a tower, does not sit down first and count the cost, whether he has enough to finish it—lest, after he has laid the foundation, and is not able to finish, all who see it begin to mock him, saying, 'This man began to build and was not able to finish.' Or what king, going to make war against another king, does not sit down first and consider whether he is able with ten thousand to meet him who comes against him with twenty thousand? Or else, while the other is still a great way off, he sends a delegation and asks conditions of peace. So likewise, whoever of you does not forsake all that he has cannot be My disciple" (Luke 14:25–33).

Then He said to them all, "If anyone desires to come after Me, let him deny himself, and take up his cross daily, and follow Me. For whoever desires to save his life will lose it, but whoever loses his life for My sake will save it. For what profit is it to a man if he gains the whole world, and is himself destroyed or lost? For whoever is ashamed of Me and My words, of him the Son of Man will be ashamed when He comes in His own glory, and in His Father's, and of the holy angels (Luke 9:23–26).

Now it happened as they journeyed on the road, that someone said to Him, "Lord, I will follow You wherever You go."

And Jesus said to him, "Foxes have holes and birds of the air have nests, but the Son of Man has nowhere to lay His head."

Then He said to another, "Follow Me."

But he said, "Lord, let me first go and bury my father."

Jesus said to him, "Let the dead bury their own dead, but you go and preach the kingdom of God."

And another also said, "Lord, I will follow You, but let me first go and bid them farewell who are at my house."

> *But Jesus said to him, "No one, having put his hand to the*
> *plow, and looking back, is fit for the kingdom of God" (Luke*
> *9:57–62).*

Jesus called people to follow Him, but He also was careful to point out the personal sacrifice involved. He challenged people to count the cost of devotion, which was subordinate of all other loyalties to serving the Lord. To hate one's family members was not a call to divorce, estrangement, or disregard, but rather, a way of saying Christ must be first and foremost in a disciple's life. The concerns of Christ must supercede the demands of any human relationship.

Jesus noted there was a cross involved for all disciples. This did not refer to a cross of crucifixion, but rather, to the yoke-like crosspiece laid on the shoulders of slaves. The crosspiece, very much like the yoke on oxen, was a symbol of total servitude. Those who desired to be disciples of Jesus were challenged to give up all rights to their own choices, decisions, and will— submitting all to the will of God.

Just as Jesus called potential disciples to count the cost, He also held out the tremendous reward for those who would accept the challenge. Disciple-ship, Jesus said, resulted in unspeakable joy and tremendous eternal benefit.

The Gospel of Luke tells us about three people who were potential disci-ples, or followers, of Jesus.

The first potential disciple came to Jesus and expressed His desire to follow Jesus because discipleship looked like a good deal to him. Jesus' disciples by that time had a degree of recognition and applause—at least in some circles—and they seemed fed and sheltered by various hosts wherever they traveled. Jesus clearly saw this man didn't really want to be a disciple. He just wanted a free meal and a little fame. Jesus sent the man away.

The second man was someone whom Jesus called directly to be a disciple and to go *preach the kingdom of God.* The man said he needed to take care of family matters first. Jesus challenged him to get his priorities right.

The third man asked to follow Jesus, but on his own terms and timing. Jesus said that to be a disciple is to have no personal terms, only acceptance of God's terms.

Jesus never said discipleship would be easy or that it involved human self-direction. Everything about discipleship was Christ-led but eternally valuable and blessed.

How do you respond to what Jesus taught about being a disciple?

Are you an observer or a genuine follower of Jesus?

Have you completely committed everything you are and everything you have to Christ? Is His will your top priority? Are His commands the basis for all your choices and decisions?

To which of the three potential disciples do you relate the most? As you seek to follow Christ Jesus, do you struggle with a need to be valued and have your needs satisfied to your liking, with a need to balance competing demands for your affection or attention, or with a need to be in charge and set your own priorities?

A
Application for Today

We live in a world that seems to spawn a new hero, a new leader, a new star, or a new trendsetter every other minute.

Of whom are you a fan? For how long?

Whom do you like to read, listen to, or watch? How much and how often?

Whom do you follow? With what degree of intent or conviction?

We might like to say we are independent of fads and trends and popular celebrities, but in reality, we all tend to devote a significant amount of time to staying up on the latest antics or accomplishments of the best-known people in whatever arena we enjoy and they occupy—sports, politics, entertainment, science, adventure, business, and yes, religion.

We all turn to other people to learn from them and in the process, we all adopt the mannerisms and style of others we admire and consider to be models of the life we'd like to lead.

Think about one specific person, other than Jesus, whom you admire and respect a great deal. Focus on a person who has the character qualities you'd like to display and the lifestyle you'd like to enjoy. If that person offered you a six-month mentorship, would you take it? Would you take it if it meant moving to another location by yourself and without any certainty of income?

What if the mentorship was for a period of ten years? What would you be willing to give up, and for how long, to be in the near presence of your most admired person? What type of reward or outcome would have to be guaranteed before you would undertake a prolonged mentorship?

Now put yourself on the other side of the mirror. Who is following in *your* footsteps? Who is copying what you do and say?

S
Supplementary Scriptures to Consider

Deep inside, most people want to be the greatest:

> *Then a dispute arose among them as to which of them*
> *would be greatest. And Jesus, perceiving the thoughts of*
> *their heart, took a little child and set him by Him, and said*

to them, *"Whoever receives this little child in My name*
receives Me; and whoever receives Me receives Him who
sent Me. For he who is least among you all will be great"
(Luke 9:46–48).

• How much more difficult is it to serve the *least* person you know, than
to be served by that person?

• In what ways are faithfulness in following Christ and service to other
people inseparably intertwined?

Deep inside, every person wants to have *spiritual power:*

> *Then the seventy returned with joy, saying, "Lord, even*
> *the demons are subject to us in Your name."*
> *And He said to them, "I saw Satan fall like lightning from*
> *heaven. Behold, I give you the authority to trample on*
> *serpents and scorpions, and over all the power of the enemy,*
> *and nothing shall by any means hurt you. Nevertheless do*
> *not rejoice in this, that the spirits are subject to you, but*
> *rather rejoice because your names are written in heaven"*
> *(Luke 10:17–20).*

- Are we more concerned about God's gift of salvation to us than the spiritual gifts He allows to flow through us?

- After a person has accepted Jesus as Savior their salvation is secure and their name is permanently and irrevocably *written in heaven*. However, God will allow various difficulties and trials to come our way to cause dependence upon Him and to grow us up in our faith and understanding of Him. It is important for us to *always* focus on what God does for us and in us each day rather than resting on the fact of our salvation. Have you considered the importance of guarding your faithfulness to God as an expression of thanksgiving for what He does *in* us, rather than letting our faithfulness become dependent on what God does *through* us?

Watchfulness and faithfulness go hand in hand:

> *"Let your waist be girded and your lamps burning; and you yourselves be like men who wait for their master, when he will return from the wedding, that when he comes and knocks they may open to him immediately. Blessed are those servants whom the master, when he comes, will find watching. Assuredly, I say to you, that he will gird himself and have them sit down to eat, and will come and serve them. And if he should come in the second watch, or come in the*

third watch, and find them so, blessed are those servants. But know this, that if the master of the house had known what hour the thief would come, he would have watched and not allowed his house to be broken into. Therefore you also be ready, for the Son of Man is coming at an hour you do not expect" (Luke 12:35–40).

• What does it mean to you to *watch* for the Lord's return?

• Are you anticipating the Lord's return soon? Are you ready if it should happen today? In the next hour? What would you need to do to become ready?

• What impact does watching for the Lord's imminent return have on a person's faithfulness?

Our being faithful is not dependent on the faithfulness of others:

> *Then one said to him, "Lord, are there few who are saved?"*
>
> *And He said to them, "Strive to enter through the narrow gate, for many, I say to you, will seek to enter and will not be able. When once the Master of the house has risen up and shut the door, and you begin to stand outside and knock at the door, saying, 'Lord, Lord, open for us,' and He will answer and say to you, 'I do not know you, where you are from,' then you will begin to say, 'We ate and drank in Your presence, and You taught in our streets.' But He will say, 'I tell you I do not know you, where you are from. Depart from Me, all you workers of iniquity.' There will be weeping and gnashing of teeth, when you see Abraham and Isaac and Jacob and all the prophets in the kingdom of God, and yourselves thrust out. They will come from the east and the west, from the north and the south, and sit down in the kingdom of God. And indeed there are last who will be first, and there are first who will be last" (Luke 13:23–30).*

• In what ways is it difficult to let God be the judge and to remain faithful to Him regardless of what others around us might say or do?

• What do these words of Jesus say to us about accepting Him as Savior and following Him as our Lord sooner rather than later?

I
Introspection and Implications

1. Do you consider yourself to be a faithful Christian? Do you rate faithfulness as an absolute? Or does faithfulness have a sliding scale of some kind? How do you believe God sees your faithfulness?

2. Do you consider yourself to be a watchful person? In what specific ways?

3. Have you ever made excuses to God for *not* doing what you believe He called you to do? What was the result?

4. How difficult is it to be steadfast in our walk with the Lord? How might we grow in our ability to be steadfast?

5. What are some of the benefits of being a Christian? Why do you follow Christ Jesus?

6. Do you ever believe God is demanding too much of you? *Can* He ever demand *too* much? To what extent do we sometimes confuse what others demand of us, or what we demand of ourselves, and what God demands of us?

7. Are you truly following Jesus as your *Lord*?

C
Communicating the Good News

Can you identify God-given opportunities where you can challenge new believers to continue to follow Jesus as *Lord* of their lives?

How might we better encourage others in the body of Christ to be faithful?

How might we better encourage others in the body of Christ to be watchful?

Notes to Leaders
of Small Groups

As the leader of a small discussion group, think of yourself as a facilitator with three main roles:

• Getting the discussion started

• Involving every person in the group

• Encouraging an open, candid discussion that remains focused on the Bible

You certainly don't need to be the person with all the answers! In truth, much of your role is to ask questions, such as:

• What impacted you most in this lesson?

• What part of the lesson did you find troubling?

• What part of the lesson was encouraging or insightful?

• What part of the lesson would you like to explore further?

Express to the group at the outset of your study that your goal as a group is to gain new insights into God's Word—this is not the forum for defending a point of doctrine or a theological opinion. Stay focused on what God's Word says and means. The purpose of the study is also to share insights of how to apply God's Word to everyday life. *Every* person in the group can and should contribute—the collective wisdom that flows from Bible-focused discussion is often very rich and deep.

Seek to create an environment in which every member of the group feels free to ask questions of other members to gain greater understanding. Encourage group members to voice their appreciation to one another for new insights gained, and to be supportive of one another personally. Take the lead in doing this. Genuinely appreciate and value the contributions each person makes.

You may want to begin each study by having one or more members of the group read through the section provided under "Bible Focus." Ask the group specifically if it desires to discuss any of the questions under the "Application for Today" section, the "Supplemental Scriptures to Consider" section, the "Introspection and Implications" and "Communicating the Good News" section. You do not need to come to a definitive conclusion or consensus about any question asked in this study. Rather, encourage your group if it does not have a satisfactory Bible-based answer to a question that the group engage in further asking, seeking, and knocking strategies to discover the answers. Remember the words of Jesus: "Ask, and it will be given to you; seek, and you will find; knock, and it will be opened to you. For everyone who asks receives, and he who seeks finds, and to him who knocks it will be opened" (Matthew 7:7–8).

Finally, open and close your study with prayer. Ask the Holy Spirit, whom Jesus called the Spirit of Truth, to guide your discussion and to reveal what is of eternal benefit to you individually and as a group. As you close your time together, ask the Holy Spirit to seal to your remembrance what you have read and studied, and to show you ways in the upcoming days, weeks, and months how to apply what you have studied to your daily life and relationships.

General Themes for the Lessons

Each lesson in this study has one or more core themes. Continually pull the group back to these themes. You can do this by asking simple questions, such as, "How does that relate to _____?", "How does that help us better understand the concept of _____?", or "In what ways does that help us apply the principle of _____?"

A summary of general themes or concepts in each lesson follows:

Lesson #1
GOD WORKS THROUGH ORDINARY LIVES
The love and value God places on each person
The uniqueness of each person's role and identity

The importance of blessing—from parents, from mature believers

The role of affirmation and encouragement in evangelism

The role of affirmation in spiritual growth

Lesson #2
JESUS CALLS ORDINARY PEOPLE TO FOLLOW HIM

The call of God on each person's life

The importance of seeing other people as God sees them

Awe of God vs. fear of God

Lesson #3
JESUS HEALS AND DELIVERS ALL WHO COME TO HIM

The role of miracles, signs, and wonders in preaching and teaching the gospel

What it means to have compassion on those in need

The prerequisites of prayer and preaching/teaching before miracles, signs, and wonders

The authority of Jesus over all manner of sickness and disease

Lesson #4
JESUS HAS COMPASSION ON SINNERS AND OUTCASTS

God's mercy

God's grace

Inclusion in and exclusion from the family of God

God's redemptive power

Lesson #5
JESUS EMPHASIZES LOVE AND FORGIVENESS TO ALL

Man's law of reciprocity vs. God's law of generosity

Breaking cycles of vengeance

Lesson #6
JESUS SEEKS OUT ALL WHO WERE LOST

Repentance

Confession

Rebellion and restoration

Freedom in Christ vs. living according to Christian ethics and the highest standards of morality and integrity

Lesson #7
JESUS TEACHES FAITHFULNESS AND WATCHFULNESS

Faithfulness

Watchfulness

Steadfastness

NOTES